How To Train Your Dog To Use A Dog Clicker

The Ultimate Beginner's Guide to Helping You Train Your Dog to Learn New Commands

Sally Tara Allen

Copyright © 2022 by Sally Tara Allen

All rights reserved. No part of this publication may be reproduced, distributed, or transmitted in any form or by any means, including photocopying, recording, or other electronic or mechanical methods, without the prior written permission of the publisher, except in the case of brief quotations embodied in critical reviews and certain other non-commercial uses permitted by copyright law.

ISBN: 978-1-63750-328-7

Table of Contents

HOW TO TRAIN YOUR DOG TO USE A DOG CLICKER 1

INTRODUCTION 5

CHAPTER 1 11

    A Brief Overview of Dog Clicker Training 11

    Dog Clicker Training Requirements 11

    Tips for using a Clicker to Train a Dog 11

        The Clicker Myths 13

CHAPTER 2 16

    Dog Clicker Training: Steps to make it Work well with Your Dog 16

    Clicker vs Marker to Train Dogs 17

    Getting to know the Clicker Better 18

        Clicker Training and Preparation Training 18

        Using clickers to record and influence behavior 19

        How do You Teach with a Clicker? 20

        Instructional Strategies for Effective Clicker Training 21

        Clicker Training Troubleshooting 22

        How do You Teach Your Dog with a Clicker? 22

CHAPTER 3 27

    Pros and Cons of Dog Clicker Training 27

        The Advantages of using a Clicker to Train Your Dog 28

        Disadvantages of Dog Clicker Training 31

        The Advantages and Disadvantages of Dog Clicker Training Summary ... 36

CHAPTER 4 38

    The Best Way To Train Your Dog Using A Clicker 38

    How do You Teach Your Dog with a Clicker? 48

        Getting Your Dog ready for Clicker Training 48

        Training Your Dog with a Clicker 51

CHAPTER 5 55

    Buyer's Guide to the Best Clickers 55

CLICKERS FOR DOG TRAINING: THE BEST OF THE BEST 56
TOP FIVE BEST CLICKERS FOR DOGS 61
HAVING ALL OF YOUR DOG'S CLICKERS IN ONE PLACE 66
HOW DID I CONDUCT RESEARCH FOR DOG CLICKER TESTING? 67
    How You Hold the Clicker matters *69*
    Dog Clickers Preferred by Trainers *70*

Introduction

You've likely heard of dog clickers, but if you want to learn how to train your dog to use one, then you'll need to learn how to do it correctly. In this book, I show you exactly how to get started.

Many people buy dog training products that they don't know anything about or which are ineffective. This guide will teach you everything you need to know about using dog clickers to train your dog in a concise way without any fluff. It is a guide that is designed to help you to train your dog to learn new commands using dog clicker. Whether it is a puppy or a mature adult dog, you can learn to use a dog clicker.

When I first got started training my dogs, I didn't know much about dog training. I had heard people saying it takes a while to teach a dog anything. I felt like I'd failed at training my dog, and was going to have to get another dog. Then one day, I came across the "clicker" and realized I didn't need another dog at all. With this amazing dog training kit/device, it is possible to train a dog to learn a new command in less than a week. This is the fastest method for teaching a dog any new command. Once you learn how to teach your dog to perform basic obedience commands, you will have a great foundation for building on your dog's learning ability.

Dogs have become an important part of people's lives. But for some dog owners, training a dog to do something useful is a daunting task. Whether it is teaching your dog to stop chewing your sofa, walk on a leash, or sit on command, you will need the right dog training tools to get the job done. This guide will teach you everything you need to know about dog training so that you can successfully train your dog and teach him new commands.

Dogs click on command. This is the main reason why dog trainers use clickers. Dog training can seem like a daunting task for the average dog owner, but using a clicker will not only help to teach your dog new commands, but also help you to teach them how to behave around other animals.

The key to training your dog is to be patient, consistent, and firm. These three qualities will help you train your dog to use a dog clicker and get him to learn new commands.

What is a Dog Clicker?

It is a training tool specifically designed to help teach your dog new commands and make them use their own natural instincts.

Clickers are used by dog trainers to teach a variety of commands, including sit, stay, down, come, heel, roll over, and so much more. Most people have seen a clicker in use during their dog training sessions, and they may even have used one themselves. However, they do not know what it is or why it is used.

What is the Purpose of a Dog Clicker?

A clicker is used for two primary reasons. The first purpose is to help your dog learn new commands. Clickers are an extremely useful tool that can be used to teach almost any command, including:

- Sit
- Down
- Stay
- Come
- Heel
- Roll over
- Leave it

- Shake
- Freeze

The second purpose of using a clicker is to help you train your dog in a natural way. A clicker makes it easy for you to train your dog while eliminating distractions like other dogs, people, and distractions in your home.

How Does a Dog Clicker Work?

A clicker works by using the same method that your dog's brain uses to learn things. When your dog hears a click sound, he will be conditioned to think that the click sound means *"attention."* The click is used to get your dog's attention, and then you can teach him what you want him to do.

Dog training, dog clicker training, or any dog training in general is a very easy and simple process that can be done anywhere at anytime. So if you are wondering how to train your dog to use a dog clicker, don't worry because this bookwill give you all the concise information you need to know about this amazing training tool.

This book will teach you the basics of dog clicker training and help you to understand how to train your dog to use a dog clicker.

Does your dog respond to commands without the reward of a treat?

When you use a "dog clicker" to get your dog to do what you want, it will become a part of your dog's brain.

There are many ways to use the clicker to teach your dog special skills, such as retrieving items from an empty bucket or performing tricks. You can also use the clicker to teach your dog basic obedience commands, such as "come" and "sit."

Getting the hang of dog clicker training can take some time, but the results are well worth the effort! Isn't it amazing how it works on your own dog, too?

The term "dog clicker training" refers to a type of canine training based on the operant fitness of bridging stimuli (the clicker). Conditioning reinforcers, such as a trainer's ability to deliver conditioning reinforcers swiftly and correctly, are used as a training tool.

Originally, the term "clicker" referred to a little mechanical noisemaking device manufactured from a child's toy that a trainer used to identify the appropriate behavior. Clickers aid in training new behaviors because they help dogs recognize the specific actions that lead to a reward.

Trainers prefer this method, but it may be utilized with a wide range of animals, including domestic and wild pets, and even young children.

Other different noises *(such as "whistle, a cluck of the tongue, a snap of the fingers, or maybe a phrase")* or visual or other sensory clues *(such as touch, hand motions, or vibrating collar)* might be used instead of a click to identify the desired behavior *(especially excellent for **deaf dogs**)*.

What if you don't want to reward your dog for obeying your commands? If so, you might want to check out this new book on dog clicker collar training.

If you want to educate your dog to love and respect you, even if it means giving up food or rewards, this dog clicker training book is for you.

Chapter 1

A Brief Overview of Dog Clicker Training

Marker training began with **B.F. Skinner's** work and was further developed by **Marion Breland Bailey, Keller Breland**, and later, **Bob Bailey** years ago.

When it comes to teaching hundreds of species, clicker training has been utilized to teach everything from fish to hermit crabs to horses and even people!

Dog Clicker Training Requirements

A dog, a clicker, and a treat pouch are all that is needed to train a dog.

Tips for using a Clicker to Train a Dog

Before you even begin training your dog, you need to work on honing your mechanical abilities.

You can *"charge the clicker"* once you've developed your mechanical prowess. Consider stocking up on a few tiny, tasty snacks. To reinforce your dog's behavior, use a clicker and then press the clicker button (*avoid clicking close to your dog's ear*), then give your dog a treat.

On the first day, collect 15 treats and split them up into

three periods of 15 treats each. When your dog is curled up across the room from you, simply press the button.

Will your dog come to you if you give him a treat?

If the response is **yes**, then the clicker is suitable and you can begin training with it. If there is a requirement to recharge the clicker, you should do so.

If your dog is afraid of the noise a hard clicker makes, try using a ballpoint pen or a snapple lid instead of a hard clicker.

Every time you click, reward your dog with a treat, preferably within the first 1-2 seconds after the click.

To put it another way, think of the clicker as your dog's income.

Clicking without rewarding your dog is a lot like getting your salary over-rolled at work. To begin with, <u>*food is a simple and effective reward*</u>. <u>*Toys and video games that your dog enjoys can be added at a later date.*</u>

It's a good idea to think of the clicker as a camera with an image of what you want your dog to accomplish. If you want to reward your dog for sitting down, click as soon as his butt touches the ground and give him a treat. If you've forgotten to click and your dog hasn't yet sat down, do it right away rather than waiting until later.

Do not provide any cues to your dog while training for clicks. It is important to keep a continual flow of positive behavior, clicks, and treats.

In return for eating the treat, the dogs will offer to sit down once more. The cue can be added at this stage. When your dog's butt touches the ground, say "sit down" and then click when he does. To get him ready for another sit-down, you can toss the treat far away from you so he has to get up and get it.

In order for him to realize the link between your instructions and his actions, he may be reluctant to sit down. Training for fluency means that your dog will respond to the cue dependably in a variety of situations, even if it is far away.

The Clicker Myths

Clicker instructors are never without a clicker or some sort of meal. A clicker can be used to teach new behaviors. The clicker is no longer necessary once the behavior has been moulded to your satisfaction.

You can gradually reduce the amount of treats you give your dog in the following stages, while still reinforcing with treats when necessary.

Instructors that use the clicker system do not penalize students for bad behavior. As a beneficial tool for moulding behavior, this won't work for self-reinforcing habits.

As a result of this combination of management, negative consequences, and corrective training, self-reinforcing manners can be dealt with by clicker trainers. Specifically, a puppy can't leap when sitting because it's not allowed to do so. Instead of focusing on the bad behavior your dog is exhibiting, clicker trainers instruct your dog to focus on what you want them to perform.

Basically, every clicker training program is exactly the same. Coaches who use a clicker and a leash may not necessarily qualify as "clicker instructors." Some dog breeds don't respond well to clicker training. No matter what breed or age, any dog can benefit from clicker training!

Do you think a clicker or your voice is more effective at identifying behavior than the other?

No way! A clicker is faster and more accurate than a verbal marker when it comes to indicating what people want dogs to do.

Chapter 2

Dog Clicker Training: Steps to make it Work well with Your Dog

At its peak in the mid-1990s, *"clicker training"* was widely recognized as a viable alternative to aversive training methods that used physical pain or fear to intimidate puppies into learning. As a result, clicker training is a kind of positive reinforcement training with a lot of technological support.

What is a clicker?

It is a training tool specifically designed to help teach your dog new commands and make them use their own natural instincts. As a *"marker,"* a clicker gives a *"click"* sound and is carried about by the user. Positive reinforcement training is based on rewarding a puppy's positive interactions with people.

We use the term *"marker"* when we notice our dog doing something right at exactly the right time. Many teachers use the phrase **"YES!"** as a marker phrase in their courses. That's why I say **"YES!"** as soon as my dog's butt hits the ground after I urge him to sit.

For me, this means that I can communicate effectively with my dog about what I enjoy about his behavior, and it eliminates the problem of having to find a reward for him that doesn't take up too much time. The behavior he used to earn the treat may have changed (toward something harmful) or he may have forgotten all about it by this point. The clicker replaces my **"YES!"** in clicker training. When I tell my dog to sit down, I click as soon as his paws touch the floor. As quickly as possible, I'll get my money back.

Clicker vs Marker to Train Dogs

Training with a clicker versus using marker words

However, there are two key distinctions between how a marker and a clicker work. There are a number of distinct reasons why clicker training is becoming so popular.

First and foremost, the sound of a clicker is distinct. It doesn't matter what kind of phrase you use as a marker. It's important that your dog hears it in a setting that isn't related to training, like when you're talking to a friend or relative.

For the most part, you won't need a clicker unless you're teaching your dog, so don't worry about getting one.

A second benefit is the clicker's realistic audio output. It's just a click; it doesn't convey happiness or sadness or any other feeling. Using a natural sound may lead to some misinterpretations or tension for your dog, but it also helps it focus better on the task at hand because it's trying to grasp the message you're communicating and your sentiments.

Getting to know the Clicker Better

Starting clicker training can be intimidating for those who have never done it before. It's difficult to get started with clicker training when you have to worry about so many other things.

In terms of use and integration, the clicker is straightforward, but it will benefit from repetition. You'll need to put in some practice before introducing your dog to clicker training.

Clicker Training and Preparation Training

Hold the clicker in one hand and press the button with the other hand. In order to get the best results, you must first understand the basics of clicker training.

To get the most out of a TV show or movie, try clicking whenever a specific actor appears on screen, or whenever a specific word is said, or in coordination with other random but regular events. Make sure you know exactly what you're about to do before you click.

Begin by pressing every time your dog stares at you; you'll soon get the hang of it. Treat yourself to something sweet after clicking. As a quick recap, the steps are as follows:

- It's possible that your dog is looking at you on his own or because you've attracted his attention.
- Do not delay in clicking and rewarding him as soon as he looks your way.

Keep doing this until you've successfully trained your dog to focus on you by rewarding him with a treat. This practice will teach your dog that the click is serious and impressive, which is a double-edged sword.

Using clickers to record and influence behavior

Giving your dog a positive response implies telling them they did a good job. For example, *if you click and reward your dog for moving close to the bed, it will be learning that you want it to lie down on the bed*. To get your dog to perform what you want him to do, you must reward him for it over and over.

To properly shape your dog, you must first take When

training your dog, you reward tiny activities that eventually lead to a larger goal by clicking and rewarding them. Make a list of the things you want your dog to do for you, such as laying down on the bed without prompting.

Make sure to reward your dog for every small step that leads to the main goal, and gradually raise your expectations.

Do not give any more rewards after you have raised your expectations. Here is a possible scenario:

Goal 1: Your dog spontaneously looks towards the bed on its own.

Goal 2: Have your dog approach the bed.

Goal 3: Your dog stands close to the bed.

Goal 4: Your dog stands on the bed.

Goal 5: Your dog sits on the bed.

Goal 6: Your dog lies on the bed.

How do You Teach with a Clicker?

Except for *"conventional teaching"* that employs techniques that intimidate, frighten, or cause distress, a clicker cannot be utilized for training that involves learning by consequence *(operant conditioning)* or learning by association *(classical conditioning)*. A dog can't be "corrected" with a clicker; it can only be used to reward good behavior.

So, a clicker can't help with issues like jumping on guests or barking, right? Not at all. These behaviors can be improved by employing the clicker, which requires you to reward your dog when he deviates from the predicted bad behavior.

Instructional Strategies for Effective Clicker Training

In the event that you lose or need to use your hands for something else, a wristbanded clicker is a good option. Carry your dinner treats in a bait bag or treat pouch.

When you only have two hands, you need a bag to keep your sweets close at hand and free up your hands for other tasks.

Don't use the clicker as a convenient remote control for your pet. If your dog does something worthy of a reward, the clicker will indicate it with a "click." Keep workouts to a minimum. For dogs, short sessions of 3–10 minutes are preferable to sessions of 30–60 minutes.

Clicker Training Troubleshooting

It's possible that your dog doesn't entirely comprehend what you expect of it if it's having trouble with a specific behavior. My dog may not understand if I lower my hand to the floor with my palm facing down as a request to lie down until I explicitly clarify it more explicitly.

The alternative would be to not expect my dog to lie down when I lower my hand, but instead to abandon the requirements that I start by clicking and rewarding every time my dog follows my hand to sit towards the floor. Once my dog has mastered this, I'll be able to raise the bar by having him lay down and raise one paw at the same time, which I'll click and praise. My expectations may rise to the point where I ask my dog to lay down with me completely.

How do You Teach Your Dog with a Clicker?

Positive reinforcement, such as clicker training, is very frequent. A clicker, a metal device in a little plastic box that generates a piercing sound when pressed, is used in this simple and effective teaching method. Saying *"good dog"* is slower and less precise than using a click, but it is less effective than simply rewarding your dog with treats.

In order to make the click meaningful to the puppy, it's important that a treat be delivered shortly after the click. The clicker becomes a conditioned reinforcer when the dog recognizes the beneficial benefits of the clicking sound. The majority of large pet retailers carry clickers, and they're usually reasonably priced.

When you use a clicker, you may teach your dog how to respond. Next, you'll progress to more complex training, which is known as "introducing" the clicker, using a step-by-step approach.

Training using a clicker should be linked to rewards.
It is not meant to totally replace the use of treats with clicker training. As a result, your dog is immediately reminded that it has earned a reward thanks to the sound of the *"click."* To emphasize this, clicks should be followed by rewards on a regular basis. Otherwise, the clicker's effectiveness will quickly wane. If you're going to be using a clicker trainer, you're going to have to treat your dog every time they click. At this level of training, it's crucial to frequently utilize strong rewards, and cookies are the most powerful reward for a puppy.

The scientific term *"operator conditioning"* explains how animals learn through the outcomes of their actions. In dog training, positive reinforcement is a common type of operant conditioning. Because you'll be giving your dog a lot of goodies, you'll want to make sure they're tasty and small enough for him to appreciate.

Use unseasoned cooked turkey or chicken parts for your training sessions if you want a simple, low-cost solution.

You should begin in a calm location.

The best place to begin training your dog is in a calm, distraction-free atmosphere. Your dog will learn best if you train him when he is hungry. Prepare some of your dog's favorite treats and the clicker.

The Clicker is introduced.

Click the button. Give your dog a goodie as soon as you push the clicker's button. This click-and-treat process should be repeated five to ten times.

Observe Your Dog.

The best way to see if you're on the right track is to click when your dog isn't looking at you. Look for a reward if your dog suddenly looks at you after the click. This means you're ready to go on to the next stage. A click-treat routine can be used if your dog doesn't yet grasp that each click is worth a treat.

Getting Started with Commands

Make use of a clicker to help you teach your dog the basics. When your dog does what you want it to do, press the clicker. After that, reward yourself with a tasty treat and express your gratitude. In the absence of the correct timing, your dog will be unsure as to why they are being given a reward.

Precision is one of the benefits of utilizing a clicker. When your dog does anything, you click and reward it. This not only helps your dog understand what it is doing, but it also makes it more willing to repeat the activity when asked to do so in the future.

Advance to Clicker Training for More Complex Exercises.

The use of a clicker might also be advantageous for more advanced instruction. Walker advises, "Just click for modest steps toward the behavior and work with your dog to finish it." Because of this, you are free to let go (aside from providing the reward, of course). To speed things up, you don't need to force your dog into a certain position. " In general, the clicker is a useful tool for the class. Consider using a clicker to train your dog to be more obedient and learn how it works for you.

Problems and Proofing Behaviour

When using a clicker for dog training, one typical mistake is over-praising your dog. Aside from the fact that your dog responds to the clicker, it also wants your approval when it does a task.

Don't underestimate a dog's need for affection and praise from its owner. Dogs with low food drives or who aren't motivated by treats won't benefit from clicker training, which is based on reward.

You'll also need precise hand-eye coordination and entire focus on the clicker if you're using clicker training for more complex actions or activities. If you can't, doing so will confuse your dog and lead to shoddy training.

Chapter 3

Pros and Cons of Dog Clicker Training

By employing a distinct click sound, you may teach your dog new skills by using a dog clicker training strategy that works. Because it's difficult to reproduce in its natural habitat, hearing it is a gratifying experience each time. You can make this sound by pressing a handheld device that makes a clicking sound when you do so. One of the most popular methods for teaching a dog pleasant behaviors is clicker training.

When a dog is able to link the clicker's sound to a tasty reward, it works. You'll begin by pressing the clicker and rewarding your dog whenever he complies with your commands. Say "sit" and reward your dog for following your instructions. If your dog sits when you command him to, use the clicker to reward him for his good behavior. You can then go through the same process for any other commands you want to teach your dog.

Your dog will eventually learn to associate the sound with a good deed. Once your dog has mastered the commands, you can stop rewarding him for every good deed without diminishing the value of the prize. There is a built-in expectation of obtaining a compliment with every click. As a result, it's a really sensible choice indeed.

Clicker training works for some dogs and doesn't for others, so weighing the benefits and drawbacks is essential to determining if this strategy is right for you and your dog.

The Advantages of using a Clicker to Train Your Dog

1. **Formalized paraphrase:** It's a great way to get your dog motivated. When you associate the clicker with the anticipation of a reward, you're establishing a favorable environment for your dog to learn and follow commands. Your dog may become open to learning about this new technique if it shows an interest in trying it out. As a result, employing this marker as a basis for a reward has been shown to be quite successful. As a result of positive feedback from clicker training, some dogs are always looking for new ways to learn new things.

2. **This training method can be used almost anywhere:** You are making your dog's day each time you click and give him a treat, since he will receive many compliments

and treats. Neither clicking nor giving treats should be done concurrently. Once you've clicked, give the treat. Tossing the reward on the floor and pushing the clicker just as your dog begins to eat it is an additional method of teaching your dog new behaviors. If you'd prefer to workout at home, you can do so while seated, standing, or even moving around. When you use this method, your dog will learn that it may be complimented in any situation. Using the clicker shows your dog that what it is doing is correct.

3. **Clicker training also works well together with other markers:** There are a number of different markers you may use with dog clicker training, and they all function well together. Whistles are sometimes used by pet trainers to reward good behavior. When complimenting your dog, even a single word like "yes" or "good" can be utilized as a signal.

Using verbal markers instead of the clicker is an option if your dog is terrified by the sound of the clicker. To communicate effectively with your dog, you'll need to employ language that's distinct from the usual speech you use. It's best not to use your dog's name as a reward marker.

4. **Don't procrastinate on the reward with clicker training:** When you utilize a clicker as your training marker, your dog will receive an immediate reward at every step of training. When your dog does anything right, he will immediately know that he has done so correctly, and this will help to encourage his excellent behavior. Due to dogs' natural desire to please their humans, the immediate reward can be an effective motivator for some. There's no doubt that the training and rewards are making dogs happy, because even dogs with a lot of energy respond positively to the immediate reward. Moreover, this can make your dog feel more at ease when it comes to further training.

5. **It is possible to eliminate any unwanted misinterpretations if you use your voice as a marker:** If you are using your firmness and non-verbal body movements, this might prevent your dog from obtaining the treat. When you use a clicker, you eliminate any variations that your dog might pick up on when you give him the incentive. Dogs may find it difficult to interpret

changes in your voice tone, especially if several people are involved in the behavior modification. With the clicker, the sound will always be the same, so there will be no confusion.

6. **Other people can help you train your dog:** Using your gadget, other people can help you train your dog if your dog responds to the sound of the clicker. If you don't have the time to educate your dog yourself, you can pay a behavioral specialist to do it for you. If you work with a huge breed like a Great Dane, St. Bernard, or Newfoundland, your spouse can help you control the atmosphere. When someone compliments your dog's wonderful behavior, your dog won't be confused if the technique for obtaining a click is the same. The clicker will elicit obedient behavior from your dog.

Disadvantages of Dog Clicker Training

Dog clicker training has a number of drawbacks, including the following:

1. **It could become a pricey venture for some dogs:** As long as the dog hasn't learned that the clicker can also signify "Good one, well-done," clicker training is

extremely effective with dogs. Even with senior dogs, this strategy works if you provide them with quality goodies as a form of reinforcement. This means that for dogs that are older and of more expensive breeds, more substantial treats are needed. A complete box of bone pieces can be consumed in a matter of days if you're trying to correct a bad habit.

2. **There are certain dogs that do not respond to the sound of the clicker:** When it comes to using a clicker for exercise, there are certain dogs who aren't fans of the sound. Make sure you don't use your dog's collar as a remote control to switch your dog on or off by not pointing the clicker at him. Before you click, make sure it's close to or behind you.

Muting the sound of the clicker may help you figure out how to improve matters if you are still getting a negative reaction from your dog. It's possible to test out clickers with quieter tones before purchasing them. Attempting to utilize dog clicker training on a dog that has never heard the sound of a clicker may not yield the results you are expecting. As a result, you may want to look into a different training strategy.

3. **This training method must be used with precision:** Because you want your dog to acquire a favorable attitude toward the clicker and associate it with something it enjoys *(a treat),* you should train with a degree of precision that isn't uncommon for other training methods. You should only use the clicker during training if you are certain that your dog will heed your directions. Once you have used the clicker, you must offer your dog a treat. Even a single unintended click can have a favorable impact on a difficult-to-change behavior.

Reward your dog every time he sits and use the clicker to reinforce the behavior. Once you've noticed that your dog has returned to its original position, simply repeat the procedure. Once your dog understands this command, you can continue on to the next task. Having to start from scratch is possible if you click too soon.

4. **In order for this strategy to work, your dog must have a strong desire for food or a toy:** Working with a dog that doesn't value rewards or for which there isn't something worthwhile to use as a reward will make this strategy difficult. What a dog craves must be something

that you can provide him with a simple click of the mouse. After every meal, you could take a short stroll to get some activity in, but it's not a good training method.

5. **The new behaviours developed with the dog clicker training are prone to be abandoned:** Dog clicker training can lead to abandoned behaviors if it is not done appropriately, especially when transitioning to a reward-based training model. If the motivation for the reward is low, random reinforcements can be difficult to apply. As a result, your dog's good behavior or training may begin to wane as a result of this. To make matters more difficult, domestic dogs are used to receiving incentives for every action they take. Your dog may revert to its old methods of doing things because they can no longer *"manipulate"* you into feeding them rewards on a constant basis.

6. **Advanced training is reguired by first timers:** In order to perform advanced activities, the first-time user of dog clicker training must have a lot of experience and expertise. It's up to you what you want your dog to learn. With basic instructions such as *"Sit down, stay, and come back,"* you can get away with a few imperfect clicks.

Using this strategy, you'll need good hand-eye coordination if you're working on more difficult exercises or behaviors. If you're unsure how to react to an exercise, you should use one of these distinct training options first.

7. **There may be conditioning issues with dog clicker training:** One of the problems that some dog owners have with clicker training is that their dog may grow conditioned to the sound of the clicker. A dog may refuse to obey a command until it first hears the sound of a reward. You can begin to wean some dogs from this behavior by linking the sound of your voice with the sound of the clicker, although this method is not always 100% effective. Your dog's response to the clicker should be reduced when you see that it is occurring more frequently.

8. **It can be difficult to control:** Sometimes it can be difficult to control, especially if you're teaching a huge dog using a clicker. As a trainer, you'll occasionally need to carry all three of these items at once. As soon as you see the desired outcome, your clicker will be in your other hand, so you don't have to worry about multitasking functions that can delay your training. If you have a large

dog, you may need a partner to help you through the process. Make sure you use a clicker that can fit around your finger or wrist if you're prone to awkward behavior. In spite of the fact that you will still need to control everything, multitasking can be reduced.

The Advantages and Disadvantages of Dog Clicker Training Summary

You can use dog clicker training to create a sound that your dog associates with a reward once you've *"charged"* these devices. There's no way your dog will get the message if you use a clicker in your house. After a few days, your dog may have picked up the idea that *"click"* means *"reward."* If you can convince yourself of this, the advantages of using this strategy will far outweigh the drawbacks.

The sound can frighten certain dogs. In dogs who have been rescued, clickers may have been used inappropriately in the past. This training strategy should be abandoned if it consistently produces a negative reaction. Stressed or scared dogs will not react well to clicker training.

When it comes to determining if your dog has a food or toy drive, the benefits and disadvantages of dog clicker training are critical. You're sending a healthy message to your pet every time it hears the sound: *"You are an excellent pet! The treats are all yours!* This kind of encouragement encourages more precise training. Each click is equated to some sort of benefit in this method as well. Before getting started with this method, there are some costs to bear in mind.

Chapter 4
The Best Way To Train Your Dog Using A Clicker

(Applicable to cats, birds, rats, and almost any kind of pet)

Make sure you're on time:

Nothing about this step involves the dog; it is entirely about you. When you observe anything you'd like your pet to repeat, practice clicking until you're comfortable doing it. For the first several weeks, you'll need to train on your own. Toss a ball into the air with a pal (or do it yourself). When the ball reaches its highest peak, press the **"Ctrl-C" key**. Count how many times you can comfortably press the button when the ball is at its highest point. You'll have excellent clicker timing when you're able to achieve this.

Find the best bargains:

Find a selection of scrumptious food. There are a slew of tasty options for training rewards. You can also use a piece of freshly prepared turkey or chicken. Several of my friends' dogs have a particular fondness for oranges and bananas.

Your dog should get a taste of a treat before he or she is ready to work for more by using something small and soft. In order to avoid kidney failure in dogs, do not use grapes, raisins, or currants in your pet's diet.

If your dog is not food-motivated, toys make fantastic treats. However, toys take time to deliver, so treats are preferable at this point. You may need to select a fairly high-value treat to attract your dog's attention.

Charge the clicker's battery:

If your dog does not appear to be frightened or startled by the clicker, you can skip this stage and proceed to the next step. The sound of a click can be helpful if your pet is hesitant or unfamiliar with you. *"Charging the clicker"* is the term for this. No matter what kind of sign you're using instead of the clicker, make sure you charge it as well.

Your dog will not understand the significance of the click at first. Clicking and treats go hand in hand in this step, so you're not seeking any specific behavior from your dog.

When your dog is doing anything you don't like, such as jumping, barking, or whining, you must be careful not to click. In practice, it's rather straightforward. The clicker can be muffled with your hands or a sock if your dog is startled by the sound. Then, click, treat, pause, and repeat as needed. If you alternate short and long breaks between clicks, this will assist your dog in learning that the click is a signal for a treat.

Repeat the process of clicking and treating between 10 and 15 times, taking a break, and then repeating the process a few hours later. As soon as your dog begins to search for a treat after hearing the click, it is time to move on to the next step of training. Now, you'll have to educate your dog on how to get you to click on its command.

Start by introducing a new habit:

You're now ready to instruct a behavior using a technique known as *"shaping."* Whenever you form, your dog is learning that she can influence you to click and reward her. By demonstrating this first behavior, you are also teaching your dog how to learn from you.

Begin by reading over the following instructions in full before moving on. It's possible to progress faster through the steps if your dog is ahead of the game, but only if you understand where you're heading first! Teaching a dog to aim a wooden dowel *(the "target")* with a piece of tape is one of the best behaviors to teach at this stage. Why?

When you are trying to teach a new behavior to a dog, it is common for the dog to provide a behavior that they are familiar with. One of the most powerful clicker behaviors is the very first one. If the prop is missing, she won't be able to perform this act. So, she'll need to come up with something else. Your first clicker-trained behavior could be for your dog to look at you. By using the wooden dowel as an anchor, you can train your dog to gently turn on light switches with his nose, stay in the contact zones during agility, close doors and be adorable while chasing a ball around the house and yard. The targeting behavior won't be given a cue until much later, so keep that in mind (see below). You want your dog to figure out how to get you to click right now. So, keep your mouth shut until you want to commend someone.

Approach the possibility with the prospect hidden behind your back, if possible. Do not use two hands for a single task.

Then, hold the target out to your dog. Click and treat if she makes even the slightest move toward it, such as sniffing, turning her head, or flicking her ears. Your dog's treat is a great opportunity to hide the target from your dog's view. Then do it again. Repetition is key.

Finally, treat them to something lavish. When your dog has finished eating the treat, stop shooting and put the target away. Then get out of here. Make sure she doesn't get tired of you. Put it off till later. It could be a few hours or perhaps the next day before this happens.

Reward Yourself:

You're juggling quite a few here, aren't you? For all your hard work and patience with your dog, reward yourself. Do anything that makes you joyful, whether it's a nap, a phone call, or anything else. Not only does your dog deserve a reward, but so does everyone else.

Raise Your Criteria:

When you return to training, you can begin to increase the difficulty of obtaining food. Ask your dog to perform a more difficult task when he obeys your command without hesitation. Rather than clicking and rewarding your pet as soon as she touches the target with her paw, wait until she touches it with her muzzle. When she contacts it with her muzzle, it makes a sound. Stop her before she becomes exhausted. Move on to the next level if she appears willing to continue.

When your dog has gotten used to contacting the target, you can raise the bar again by requiring that she continue to touch it, even though it has been moved. Reward her with a reward each time she successfully reaches the target while in these new positions. Stop if she's exhausted or appears to be tiring. If not, carry on as before. Remember that we haven't yet come up with a name for this type of behavior. The cue is the target.

In the next session, after your dog has warmed up, you must touch the target close to the end. Raise Your criteria higher (and higher).

In the end, it must be done. Wait for your dog to press her nose against the target and then reward her. Holds of more than one second should only be given praise. Each time, you'll want to make it more difficult, but it won't be impossible. Make your dog's life easier by preparing him or her for success. If she tries more than twice and still doesn't get rewarded, then you've probably made the task too hard. What she used to get rewarded for is not what you want her to do.

Put the behavior into context:

You'll be able to put your dog on cue once he starts

touching the end with speed and accuracy. After saying "touch" and revealing the target, you should keep the target behind your back.

When your dog first hears the word, she won't make the connection, but after some time, she'll pick it up on the meaning. When she responds to your request to "touch," click and reward her. Take away the target from her if she touches it without first saying "touch." Start by presenting the target and saying the cue if she doesn't make contact with it in a brief period of time (*1/2 second*). When she touches you, reward her with a click and a treat.

Keep going until she touches the cue and waits for your command to offer the target when you say it. This phase can be skipped if you want her to touch the target without a cue, so that the target itself always signifies touching.

Only Reward When Necessary:

This is critical because it reduces your dog's desire to give up, even if you don't offer her a treat or praise. Slot machines are compared to soda machines in this way: If you pay for a soda and don't get anything in return, you're likely to stop using the machine. Every time you go out, you expect a soda. It's not that you expect a reward, but many people are addicted to slot machines. You can take advantage of the fact that dogs prefer to gamble, just like many people.

Focus on the ninth step. Reward your dog for each time she touches the target on cue while working on the third and fourth of four touch demands. Start paying her intermittently if she's regularly putting her nose on the target. When your dog successfully reaches the target, it's okay to simply offer her praise when she does so.

Avoid rewarding her with food or clicks. Turn around and reposition the target. When praising your dog's triumphs, give him about 50 percent of the time, but don't praise him every other time. Your dog would see a trend if you continued to do what worked in the past. Because you won't be able to reward everyone, make sure you just select the best responses.

To begin weaning your dog from the clicker, you might begin by saying "yes" and rewarding your dog instead of clicking and rewarding.

In the end, always give an excellent answer that will get you a big prize. For the grand finale, I like to scatter a few treats on the floor. While your dog is chowing down, put the clicker, treats, and target to one side and focus on the task at hand.

Travel with it:

Your dog must be able to adapt to a variety of situations. If you're going to train, it's best to do it somewhere different or with more distractions. When you change the surroundings, it becomes more difficult for your dog to follow your commands. Reduce your standards when you're in a new environment or there are additional distractions. You should check for responses that are less than flawless the first time you train in the living room instead of the bedroom. Build up to the level of perfection that you have previously achieved.

Play around with different distractions around the house to improve your game. For best results, use a combination of additional cues that your dog understands before treating. Click and treat once your dog sits, lies down, and touches the target before he sits, lies down, etc.

Your dog should be able to do a variety of combinations in the yard, on a sidewalk, or even while driving to and from a dog park. Your dog may not understand what "touch" means each time the surroundings change. Neither is she being stubborn or willful in this instance. In this new context, your dog has no understanding of what you mean.

If you've forgotten how to shape something, just go through the process again. You'll feel like you're on fast forward with her. Keep the sessions brief and fun, as usual. Never fail to leave on a high note.

If you want to teach your dog to focus on your hand while on a walk, you can follow the same basic procedures indicated above for shaping. You can teach your dog everything from sounding an alarm bell when it's time to go outside to whirling around in circles to chasing a ball and barking on command. Be inventive!

Using the clicker in combination with luring and capturing is also an option. The target or a small amount of food can be used as a lure to induce your dog to perform the desired behavior. Begin utilizing shaping to complete the behavior as quickly as possible. When your dog performs a complete behavior, you click and treat him. If you want to teach your dog to stretch, for example, observe when and where she naturally stretches, and then say "stretch" and click and treat when she does. Soon she'll begin to provide it more frequently. Every time, try to say the cue before, or at least while stretching, and then click and treat. Another smart way to employ capture is to get your dog to look at you when you approach.

How do You Teach Your Dog with a Clicker?

The greatest way to educate and reward your pet's positive behavior is to use a clicker. Both you and your dog will have a good time, and regular training will yield quick and noticeable improvements. The basic premise that a dog will continue to perform any activity that is rewarded is at the heart of clicker training. It would be much easier for you to teach your dog new skills if he understood what the first clicker was all about.

Getting Your Dog ready for Clicker Training

It's important to become proficient in the use of a clicker. A clicker is a little plastic gadget with a button or a small metal piece that you press down to make a clicking sound.

For best results, you must use a clicker at the proper time and place when your dog performs an expected action. Be sure that there is some kind of reward for every time you hear a click *(e.g., food, toys, compliments)*.

Because the clicker is used to communicate to your dog that there will be a reward rather than praise, you need to be aware of this fact.

Use a clicker to help your dog learn two important things: the exact moment that she's doing the right thing and that a reward always follows the click. Using a clicker instead of verbal cues *(such as "good" or "thank you")* is thought to be a more efficient way to communicate with your dog during an exercise.

You may locate the clicker like the winning buzzer on a casino game show. The sound is a signal that the proper behavior or action has been carried out at the right time.

Pippa Elliott, a qualified veterinary technician, advises: "It's a unique sound, unlike anything else your dog hears, so we use a clicker to communicate with him." The click of a ballpoint pen withdrawing or a click with your tongue can be used, as long as it is consistent.

The clicker should be introduced to your dog. You must first educate your dog on how to utilize the clicker before you can use it for training. Clicker *"charging"* refers to this. Keep the treat in one hand and the clicker in the other when you are in a calm room with your dog.

To begin, press the button once. Give your dog a treat as soon as he performs for you and you hear the click.

For the sake of efficiency, you'll need at least a few treats. Keep doing this over and over. When you hold the treat in your hands before pushing the clicker, your dog will not begin to anticipate when the treat will arrive.

Keep your hands closed and activate the clicker only when your dog has stopped sniffing and reaching for the treat. Watch your dog's reaction to the clicker to see how responsive he is. It is possible that certain dogs are sensitive to the clicker's sound. It's possible that the sound of the clicker is too loud for your dog. You might use a towel to muffle the clicker's sound. Instead of a mouse, consider using a ballpoint pen, which makes a quieter clicking noise.

Verbal instructions will be necessary if he continues to flee from the clicker's sound.

Training Your Dog with a Clicker

You should look for a peaceful area: Use the clicker to educate your dog to heed commands after he becomes used to the clicker's sound *(e.g., sit down, lie down, stand)*. It may be preferable to teach him in a calm, distraction-free location, away from other people. Outdoor training may be an option for those who have a fenced-in backyard. To help your dog feel more comfortable with clicker training, you may choose to use the clicker in a more noisy or distracting environment *(e.g., in a room with the TV on or in a dog recreation park)*.

Click whenever your dog exhibits good behavior: When your dog is behaving in a positive way, reward him by clicking on him. To teach your dog healthy habits, you can use a clicker technique known as ***"catching,"*** in which you click when you notice your dog doing something that he's already mastered on his own. You can reward him for lying down by, for example, clicking and tossing him a treat right afterward. Make sure to repeat the process as soon as he stands up to eat the treat. In order to use this strategy, your dog must already know how to behave politely without being told. Every time he performs a new behavior, use the clicker to reaffirm that he is doing it correctly and urge him to do it again.

Use the clicker at every step of a new behaviour: *"Shaping"* is the technical term for what we're doing here. By using the clicker and giving immediate praise at every opportunity, you are creating a new pattern of behavior from the ground up. As an example, if you want to teach your dog to lay down in a specific spot, click and reward him when he advances in that direction. After that, you can reward him for each small step he takes: walking to a new location, arriving at the new location, starting to lie down, and finally lying down on the floor.

In order to help him learn the new behavior, use the clicker and reward him for even the smallest accomplishments. He'll believe that the learning process is enjoyable, and he'll be anxious to try out the new habit. When learning a new skill, you may want to practice each step over and over before moving on to the next level.

Use a food lure: You can get your dog to do something good by offering him a tasty treat first. When teaching a dog to lie down, it is common to use a food lure. Because of this, you will begin by placing the reward directly in front of your dog's nose, and then gradually lower the treat to the floor. Your dog will keep a close eye on the treat as it descends.

Be ready to reward him as soon as his elbows touch the ground. When you notice that your dog responds consistently to the food lure, remove the food lure but keep the reward in front of his nose like a treat. Do not wait to give him the treat once he has fallen asleep. Eventually, your dog will be able to follow your hand's signals to lie down without the promise of a reward. Lures are typically more efficient than other approaches, like shaping or catching.

Make use of a verbal cue: You can use a verbal cue in conjunction with any clicker training method you want. You can give your dog the cue first and then wait for him to perform the desired action according to the cue. When he does the behavior, reward him with a treat by clicking on him.

"Sit" or *"down"* are good examples of short and direct verbal cues you can use. It would be too long to use

phrases like ***"act like a nice pup and sit still"*** or ***"Move over for mama."*** The verbal cue must be given prior to your dog altering his behavior so that he can learn to listen to your command and obey it.

Following the "lure" strategy, utilize the hand signal after you have given a verbal cue.

Chapter 5

Buyer's Guide to the Best Clickers

Choosing the right type of dog clicker will have a significant impact on your pet's training. How can you know which dog clickers are manufactured the right way when there are so many on the market?

Here are some things to think about:

- *Material*: The quality and longevity of the clicker will be affected by the material. Stainless steel is the best material to use in order to ensure that it does not rust.

- *Simplicity*: Using a clicker when there is a need for positive motivation may not be successful if it is not employed promptly. That's why an easy-to-use dog clicker is essential.

- *Accessories*: Check to see if the device includes a training manual and samples of dog treats. The help of a consumer guide makes it easy to build a close relationship with your dog.

- *Portability*: Because you'll be carrying your clicker around a lot when teaching your dog, you'll want a product that's lightweight and portable. There should be some kind of strap or flexible ring that keeps the clicker in the user's hand while they are working.

- *Design*: It's important to pick a clicker that's easy to use, so look for one with an ergonomic design. To keep your hands safe from injury, avoid sharpening the sides.
- *Clicker loudness*: Because some clickers are so loud that they can startle your dog, it is important to choose one that is appropriate for your dog's level of sensitivity. It's ideal to go with a volume that's just right—not too high, not too low.
- *Warranty*: Dog training equipment that comes with a warranty ensures that any damage or loss is covered by the manufacturer. It's also a good clue that you're getting a real product.

Clickers for Dog Training: The Best of the Best

Hand-held clickers for fluffy white dogs

My top options for dog clickers are also great for training other pets in the home. Do you have a new puppy to train?

Consider becoming a full-time dog trainer, as many trainers suggest that using clickers will help you train your dog more quickly. As a result, I put them through the ringer.

With over 100 hours of testing under my belts, I was able to give each of the 11 different dog training clickers I tested an extensive amount of time. For the purpose of answering a simple question,

- which clicker is best for training your dog?
- Is a dog training clicker something you really need?

My testing procedure is as follows: I've gathered all of my dog clickers.

This is how I tested my dog clickers: In order to determine which dog clickers were the most effective, we looked at the best dog clickers, best all-around, loudest, softest, and worst dog clickers.

Is it necessary to use a dog training clicker?

You can use a clicker to make a unique "click" sound when you press the button on a small hand-held gadget.

The mechanism of a clicker is rather straightforward. A tiny metal strip is encased in the clicker. This strip bends when you click the button. You'll hear a click as soon as you release the button.

Although a clicker is a basic and inexpensive tool, it serves a specific purpose in dog training. Imagine that you want to teach your dog a new trick: shaking! You can choose to utter **"Good," "Yes,"** or whatever word you choose to utter when your dog places its paw in your palms, as a thank you, you reward your dog with a treat. By doing this, you can teach your dogs exactly what they need to do to get a reward.

Your dog will learn to associate the reward with this sound. This sound is referred to as the "*marker*" in dog training. Rather than saying, "Good job," you hit a button. The sound of a click serves as a marking. Once your dog learns a new skill or behavior, you won't need to use a clicker as often (a clicker is used for training only).

Clicker training, as opposed to voice training, is a popular method of training dogs and it has several advantages over using a voice marker.

1. **<u>Quicker and more precise</u>**: Many people believe that pressing a button at the same moment your dog does a task is faster and more precise than pronouncing a word.

2. **A consistent tone**: the clicker's sound is the same every time it is activated. When you're sick, your voice may sound different.

You may now be asking yourself if using a clicker is really required when it comes to training your dog.

In dog training, the usefulness of employing a clicker is still up for debate. According to several studies, training dogs using a clicker accelerates their ability to learn new behaviors. The use of a clicker has been shown to be more successful, but a new study reveals that utilizing vocal instruction is just as effective.

Even if the worst-case scenario comes true, a clicker is still a useful training aid.

During training, the owner of an Australian Shepherd uses a clicker to get the dog to raise its paw in response to the click. Precision was cited as the most important factor in their decision. In addition, if you're continually barking commands at a large number of dogs, your voice can get hoarse.

While being clicker-trained, an Australian Shepherd may be seen shaking the trainer's hand. Using the clicker was my preferred method of training when I was a novice with no previous experience with dogs. Even though a clicker isn't required for training, if given the choice, I'd choose to use one instead of not using one at all, based on my own experience.

The good news is that clickers are reasonably priced; the bad news is that you don't need a clicker if you don't want to train your dog in the near future. It may surprise you to hear that clickers may be used to train a variety of animals in addition to dogs, including cats, horses, dolphins, elephants, and even children. Invest your money in the dog supplies you need. The majority of the time, clickers are used to train dogs, which is why my clicker recommendation is primarily focused on that application.

You'll need to use a dog whistle instead for training dogs over long distances, as the sound is stronger and travels further.

Clickers are in place and ready for evaluation and testing. We would never suggest anything that we ourselves wouldn't be happy to use on our own dogs. That's why we put each clicker in this guide through its paces.

When we were done, we had spent more than 100 hours analyzing the best and worst dog training clickers on the market.

Top Five Best Clickers for Dogs

There are now so many different brands of dog clickers on the market that it can be tough to know which one is best for your pet. The multiple vital features put on display by different brands of dog clickers at varying rates can leave you perplexed.

That's why you need to be familiar with the most commonly used names in the industry right now. These five brands are the greatest, in my opinion, and I've outlined why in detail below.

1. EcoCity Training Clicker: This eco-friendly dog training clicker is a top-notch option. It's a set of four with a clicker button on each, and they're both lightweight and robust. No matter how hard you try, the button won't stick. The item is one of my favorites because it makes an audible click sound. It's comfortable to hold and features a detachable strap in case you misplace it. Because it comes in four hues (red, blue, white, and black), I also appreciate the fact that it is versatile. Because it is neither too loud nor too mild, it is ideal for pets that are sensitive to noises.

A dog training manual is included in the kit to make things

a little bit easier during training. Just because the wrist strap is so small doesn't mean it's really a big deal. It's up to you whether or not you want to use it.

In addition, it has a tendency to click under low pressure, which might produce an undesirable noise. You should be aware that, because of the device's popularity, there are imitations, and you should only purchase from reputable retailers.

2. **The StarMark Clicker**: Similarly, the StarMark Clicker System is a button-style clicker that is both long-lasting and simple to operate. It features a crisp click sound that rings out frequently and is pleasing to your dog's eardrums. This is the best clicker to use if you want to be consistent in your dog's training. With the elevated button, you won't miss a single button press. Its metal construction assures its long-term viability and protects it from rust. You may also attach a keychain to it due to its ergonomic shape, which makes it easy to grip. The clicker's spherical form makes it comfortable to hold in your thumb. To give your dog a treat, simply click the button on the remote control. In this manner, it will be able to connect the praise to the actions. Experts have endorsed the use of the clicker

as a scientifically proven method of dog training. Because of this, you will be able to effortlessly and safely teach your dog. The clicker is one of the noisiest on the market, which may preclude its use with your dog. It's also a bit pricey.

3. **Karen Pryor Clik Stik:** Dog training pioneer Karen Pryor is known as the *"Mother of the Clicker"* for good reason. This is due to her role in popularizing canine training techniques in the 1990s. As a result, she appears to know what works and what doesn't with a clicker. As a result, most of Karen's dog training clickers are in high demand.

Because it comes with a retractable target stick, making it ideal for target and trick training, this is one of the best clickers for dog training. With the Clik Stik, you can train your dog with one hand free.

Because it is neither too mild nor too loud to shock your dog, the clicker is an excellent option for individuals with sensitive pets. Using it is a breeze, and it creates a clear, crisp sound. The huge elevated button makes it difficult to accidentally press it. You may attach it to a keychain or your wrist with the lanyard loop on the clicker's end. As a result, it has an ergonomic design that allows you to hold it comfortably in your hands. This implies that you won't have to juggle, drop, or lose another gadget.

The button is easy to press and does not get stuck in any position. Pet training and bonding exercises can be made a lot easier with this equipment.

Many different abilities can be taught to your dog by utilizing this device. Some examples include teaching your dog to focus and move away. The lack of a user manual is a drawback of the clicker. As a bonus, if you don't push down hard enough in the center, you may not be able to hear the clicker sound.

4. **PetSafe Clik-R Trainer**: When it comes to dog training, it's important to keep in mind that the trainer has to be just as skilled as the dog. In order to attain your training goal with clicker training, you must click precisely when the cues appear on the screen. The clicker can teach a dog a lot of things if it's used correctly.

To teach your dog new tricks, use the *PetSafe Clik-R Trainer*. It's made of plastic, yet it boasts a big, easy-to-press button. It's composed of high-quality materials, yet it's also very straightforward to use.

The clicker contains a finger grip made of elastic to keep it in your hand, as well as a hole to link it to your keychain. A finger-looped clicker is a good solution for those who have never used one before.

It's a great option for dogs who tend to yank on the leash, as it encourages them to focus on walking. The clicker's ergonomic form makes it comfortable to hold in either hand. It's ideal for training dogs indoors or in solitude because of its mellow tone.

It comes with a booklet that explains how to use the clicker. As a method to bond with your dog and teach it some new abilities, I would recommend this. As a result of the clicker's exceptionally quiet sound, it cannot be used for outdoor training.

5. **Attmu Training Clicker**: Finally, we have the Attmu Training Clicker. Small tricks, obedience, and retraining poor behavior are all possible with the Attmu Training Clicker. It's the best way to communicate with a dog without scaring him, so it's the best option. It has a mellow sound, making it ideal for use in the house or with sensitive pets.

You won't have to worry about the clicker breaking or

corrosion. Red, blue, dark, yellow, white, and orange are just a few of the hues offered. It's strong and light, too. It has a huge, easy-to-press button that makes a loud enough noise. It's safe to say that there are seven objects in each pack, so you can utilize many clickers simultaneously. The wrist strap ensures that you don't lose your clicker while you're working out. As a result, it's easier to carry around. The clicker's main drawback is that it is prone to breaking. You can, however, always replace it because it comes in a pack of seven.

Having all of Your Dog's Clickers in One Place

There are a number of different types of clickers to choose from, but most of them are simply rebranded. few examples are:

- Downtown Pet Supply.
- EcoCity.
- Good2Go.
- Karen Pryor.
- Petco.
- PetSafe.

- StarMark.
- Top Paw.

How did I Conduct Research for Dog Clicker Testing?

A deaf French Bulldog and an energetic Labrador were among the other dogs I tried out the clickers on to see how they reacted to the sound of each one. I measured the volume of each clicker using a sound meter. The higher the reading, the more obnoxious the clicker.

In the end, I did the following tests:

Durability: On a wood floor, rubber-soled shoes were used to step on each clicker.

Simpleness: The ease with which each clicker might be activated throughout training.

We chose our top options based on their strengths and weaknesses in each of these categories.

The results of our tests are shown here.

There are a few things I noticed when testing the attributes described above.

- The volume of most clickers is comparable.

- I was astonished to see a dog training clicker next to a sound meter to measure decibel levels.

Every single clicker measured within 2 decibels of each other when we tested the sound. There is a presumption here that all clickers are equally loud. When we asked our human testers to rate the loudness of each clicker, we got wildly divergent responses. We think that the real tone of each clicker, not how loud it is, is the reason why the results are so different.

Even though both clickers sounded the same to our sound meter, clickers with a tinny sound were often considered louder than those with a clean sound. Is the implication right that you can't rely on your ears to tell you how loud a clicker is?

If your dog is easily startled by loud noises, a quiet clicker is better suited for indoor training, while a loud clicker is better suited for outdoor training when your dog is far away.

To ensure that you don't lose one of your four dog clickers, you'll probably need to get four of the wrist straps in four different colors: red, blue, white, and black. There is, however, a chance of it breaking even if you don't lose anything.

- It's aggravating to try to train your dog only to realize you don't have a clicker with you.
- Once you select your preferred clicker, get an additional one. To avoid a last-minute sprint to the store, you may pre-order your pup's supplies online.
- Fortunately, there are a lot of clickers that come in three-packs or more. If you lose or break one, you'll always have a replacement at the ready.

How You Hold the Clicker matters

This might be a challenge when training your dog, because holding the leash and treats while juggling a clicker can be challenging at times. A common design of clickers is to be readily fastened onto your body. Some may be worn around your wrist, while others can be hung from your wrist using a strap that extends out from the wrist. A lanyard or keychain can be attached to a clicker that does not have these attachments.

While some attachments kept the clicker nearby, you still had to reach for it with other types of clickers I tested. My thumb was always within easy reach of the clicker because the strap kept it in my palm without needing to clasp it with my fingers.

Clickers who make your dog's tail wag

In our quest to find the finest, over 11 different dog training clickers were tested and studied by us. In light of the description I gave for the loud and quiet dog clickers category, I'd say the greatest all-around clickers are:

When it comes to the best dog clicker out there, it's the

- PetSafe Clik-R.
- Petco's Box Clicker.
- Clicker for Sodt Dogs by Good2Go.
-

Dog Clickers Preferred by Trainers

Small, easy-to-hold, and loud are the best features of a good clicker for most trainers; this is a fantastic choice because it is always within reach. In addition, a flexible strap can be attached to the back of the device to keep it in place. When it comes to clickers, I strongly recommend upgrading to one that has a finger loop.

The PetSafe Cliker is the thickest clicker I've ever tested (*it's consistently regarded as one of the best dog training clickers by the general public*). However, even with my little thumb, I was able to easily press the button. When Cliker was in my husband's enormous, meaty paws, he did just as well. You can hear it clearly, and it's loud and clear.

Loud dog clicker

Petco's clicker (*the loudest clicker we reviewed*)

Compared to other clickers, the Petco Box Clicker has a louder click. If your dog is sensitive to sound or afraid of startling noises, you should avoid using this clicker. Although modern clicker designs are more practical and easier to maintain, the original is still the loudest; instead of pressing a button, you put your finger inside the box, bending a small piece of metal. If you listen closely, you'll hear a loud click as the metal re-emerges.

The harsh plastic corners of the square form began to irritate my palm after a while of using it. It was only during longer training sessions that this issue arose. You'll want to use a loud click if your dog has trouble hearing normally. It is, however, not something I would use on a regular basis because of its clunky form factor.

Softest dog clicker

The Clicker for dog training by Good2Go Soft (the quietest clicker reviewed)

The most delicate clicker

For dogs that are easily scared by loud noises, use a calm, soothing click. The Yorkshire Terrier, is quite sensitive to noise. Her delicate Yorkie ears are startled by unexpected noises. Even though she was aware that a reward was coming, she reacted with a flinch to the majority of the clickers I tried.

Only the **Soft Clicker** had a favorable reaction to the gentler click that was used. It took a few clicks for her to get acclimated to it, but the same can be said for any dog when they are first introduced to a clicker. This clicker was four times quieter when measured with the noise meter than the next quietest one.

Even though the sound was softer, our dogs were able to immediately identify the click during training despite this. The tone may be softer, but it's still very distinct. You may need something a little louder if you're doing distance training in a busy park or open field.

The Silent Clicker

The Silent Clicker features a comparable finger strap to my top choice, allowing me to rapidly press this clicker all day long. This is one of the best clickers for noise-sensitive dogs; if your dog is afraid of loud, harsh clicks, check out this one.

That didn't make the cut: dog clickers.

To use a clicker, all you need to do is buy one and plug it in. There is a clicking sound at the end of the process. Don't assume that all of your clickers are winners. The following clickers did not measure up to our top recommendations in one way or another.

According to our tests, the aforementioned recommendations are correct.

In terms of bulk purchases, I recommend *EcoCity's Dog Training Clicker with Wrist Strap*.

You won't be disappointed with these clickers, despite their low price. Compared to the **StarMark Pro-Training Clicker Deluxe**, these may be extremely similar, yet they are perfect. The elastic strap can be attached to a belt loop or even to the clicker to create a wrist strap; the sound is loud and crisp. When it comes to a bracelet with a clicking sound, this is the best option. They're incredibly cost-effective when purchased in a 4-pack. In my opinion, the clicker's only issue is that the button can be accidentally activated by pressing it too lightly.

Clicker training is said to have been pioneered by Karen Pryor. In the 1990s, she played a key role in popularizing clicker training. The I-Click dog training clicker is the greatest. It is easy to use, with a loud and sharp sound, and the higher top button makes it less likely to be unintentionally hit. If you don't push the center of it, you can't generate a clicking sound. It is possible to link each clicker to a key chain or wrist band, but you will need to buy these separately.

There is a wristband, keychain clip, and lanyard with a carabiner attachment for the **Good2Go Dog Training Clicker**. And that's what makes this clicker so interesting. This clicker is similar to their other clickers, which we preferred because the thumb rests on the cutouts of the clicker. This clicker's teardrop shape made it comfortable to hold.